Original title:
Snowbound Peace

Author: Sara Säde
ISBN HARDBACK: 978-9908-1-1672-3
ISBN PAPERBACK: 978-9908-1-1673-0
ISBN EBOOK: 978-9908-1-1674-7

Frosted Serenity at Twilight

In twilight's glow, the snowflakes dance,
Soft whispers of joy, a fleeting chance.
With laughter ringing through the night,
We gather 'round the soft, warm light.

Candles flicker, casting dreams,
As sparkling stars erupt in beams.
Each heartbeat sings a joyous song,
In this frosted haven, we belong.

Hearty feasts upon the table lay,
As friends unite to share the day.
Filled with cheer, each smile glows bright,
In festive spirit, hearts take flight.

The air is rich with love and cheer,
As we embrace those we hold dear.
With every toast, the night unfolds,
In frosted serenity, warmth beholds.

The Calm After the Snowfall

The snowflakes dance, a gentle sweep,
Blanketing all in a silence deep.
Children laugh, their spirits bright,
Joyful echoes in the soft moonlight.

Fires gleam in windows wide,
Warmth and love, a cozy tide.
Muffins bake, the scents arise,
Laughter flickers like the skies.

Tranquility Wrapped in Winter's Touch

In the stillness, whispers play,
Snowflakes gather, bright and gay.
Branches draped in crystal white,
Nature's quilt, a pure delight.

The stars twinkle, a distant cheer,
Wrapping hearts, drawing near.
Hot cocoa swirls in playful mugs,
Every sip, a winter hug.

Whispered Secrets of the Frozen Earth

The icy breath of winter sings,
Sharing tales of hidden things.
Beneath the frost, life waits to bloom,
Patiently resting, in nature's room.

Footprints lead through gleaming snow,
Each step taken, spirits grow.
Families gather, stories unfold,
Memories cherished, more than gold.

The Still Heart of a Winter's Day

Morning light on frosted ground,
A tranquil beauty all around.
Sleds race down the hillside's curve,
Joyous moments we preserve.

Winter's breath, a quiet song,
Binding us where we belong.
Love and laughter fill the air,
In this season, hearts laid bare.

In the Heart of Frosted Tranquility

Snowflakes twirl in the soft night air,
Children laugh, with joy they share.
Lanterns glow with a gentle light,
Creating magic in the winter's bite.

Hot cocoa warms the chilly hands,
Friends gather 'round, making plans.
Laughter dances like the stars,
In this place, no one bears scars.

Frosty breath hangs in the night,
Every heartbeat, pure delight.
Warmth of love fills every heart,
In this season, never apart.

A Night Wrapped in Silver Calm

A silvery moon hangs overhead,
Whispers of winter, softly spread.
Crisp air fills the night with cheer,
Embracing all who wander near.

Glittering snow blankets the ground,
In silence, festive joys abound.
Neighbors share their holiday treat,
Joyful faces and laughter sweet.

Fires crackle in every home,
Welcoming souls who freely roam.
In this night, dreams intertwine,
Wrapped in calm, all is divine.

Winter's Quiet Embrace

Frost-kissed trees stand tall and proud,
A gentle hush blankets the crowd.
Candles flicker with warm, soft glow,
As winter's peace begins to flow.

Scarves and mittens, colors bright,
In this wonderland, pure delight.
Music echoes through the square,
Spreading joy beyond compare.

Children build their best snowman,
Creating magic as only they can.
Under stars, the world feels right,
In winter's quiet, hearts take flight.

Silent Whispers of the Frost

Morning breaks with a golden hue,
Frosty branches, sparkling dew.
Chimes ring out in the crisp air,
Carrying joy, a sweet affair.

Warm firelight beckons from inside,
Families gather, hearts opened wide.
Gifts exchanged with gleeful eyes,
In this moment, love never lies.

As night falls, the stars align,
With laughter echoing, spirits shine.
Nature's peace in chilly breath,
Silent whispers of warmth and rest.

Whispers of Winter's Serenity

Snowflakes dance on whispering breeze,
Laughter twirls around the trees.
Glistening lights adorn the night,
Hearts aglow, spirits take flight.

Mugs of cocoa, warm and sweet,
Gathered friends in bright retreat.
Songs of joy echo through the air,
Moments cherished, memories rare.

Fires crackle with a gentle cheer,
Tales of magic we hold dear.
As winter whispers, softly bright,
Each moment wrapped in pure delight.

Stars above in sparkling display,
Guide our dreams till break of day.
In winter's arms, we find our place,
Embracing joy, a warm embrace.

A Canvas Cloaked in Tranquility

Blankets white on nature's ground,
Peaceful whispers all around.
Canvas painted fresh and bright,
Soothe the heart, a pure delight.

Gentle breezes carry songs,
Of holiday cheer where joy belongs.
Children laughing, running free,
Chasing dreams beneath the trees.

Twinkling lights begin to glow,
In this world of winter's show.
Every corner, love will find,
A chance to spark and bind.

Sipping warmth by the fire's side,
Hearts connected, joy our guide.
In this canvas, calm and bright,
We celebrate this wondrous night.

The Hushed Breath of Crystal Air

Morning frost with a gentle sigh,
Whispers glide as the world goes by.
Crystal air, a sparkling show,
Each breath taken, pure and slow.

Nature holds its silent tune,
Underneath the glowing moon.
Branches sway in soft embrace,
Carried echoes fill the space.

Footsteps crunch on frosty ground,
In this stillness, peace is found.
Snowflakes glide like feathered grace,
Filling hearts in this sweet place.

In the hush, our hopes arise,
Chasing dreams beneath clear skies.
Together we weave memories fair,
In the hushed breath of crystal air.

Frosty Stillness in Lingering Twilight

Twilight whispers on frosty skies,
Colors bleed as daylight dies.
Shadows linger, soft and light,
Holding magic as day turns night.

Candles flicker in windows bright,
Embers dance, a warm delight.
Stories shared in the gathering glow,
Filling hearts with love to flow.

Frost hangs low, a sparkling veil,
Winds carry tales like a soft gale.
In this moment, peace we find,
As joy and laughter intertwine.

Crisp and clear, the world looks new,
Under twilight's enchanting hue.
Together we savor, hold on tight,
In this frosty stillness of night.

Layers of Calm in Snowy Air

Snowflakes twirl like dancers bright,
Glistening under soft moonlight.
Children laugh, their joy unfurled,
A splendid peace blankets the world.

Warm fires crackle, cocoa steams,
Inside, we share our sweetest dreams.
The quiet night, a tender spell,
In layers of calm, all is well.

Winter's Whispering Hush

Silvery frost on every tree,
Nature rests in tranquility.
Whispers float on the chilly breeze,
Winter's hush brings hearts to ease.

Stars twinkle like scattered snow,
In this stillness, love will grow.
Every moment, a gentle sigh,
As time melts softly, passing by.

A Dance on the Icebound Meadow

Skates glide swiftly, laughter soars,
A choreographed dance that explores.
Friends embrace the cold in glee,
While nature's stage is wild and free.

Footprints trace stories on frozen ground,
In winter's magic, joy is found.
With every twirl, our spirits rise,
Beneath the vast and starry skies.

The Frozen Pause of Nature's Breath

Under the weight of powdery white,
A quiet pause, a serene sight.
Branches bow with snowflakes' kiss,
In this moment, we find our bliss.

The world is hushed, a gentle plea,
To savor stillness, to just be free.
Nature sleeps, yet hearts ignite,
In frozen pauses, warmth feels right.

Resting in a White Embrace

Snowflakes dance in the crisp air,
Laughter echoing everywhere.
Warm mugs held with gentle glee,
A festive spirit, wild and free.

Children play in fields of white,
Joyful hearts gleam in the light.
Frosty breath mingles with cheer,
Winter's magic drawing near.

Twinkling lights adorning trees,
Sweet scents wafting on the breeze.
Carols sung with voices bright,
In this white embrace, pure delight.

The world a canvas, soft and smooth,
Nature's art, in every groove.
Resting in this snowy scene,
Happiness felt, a lasting dream.

The Peaceful Pulse of Winter

Hushed whispers in the falling snow,
A world transformed, soft and slow.
Fires crackle, glowing red,
While gentle thoughts swirl in our head.

Frosted windows, stories bright,
Gathered close, hearts filled with light.
In the quiet, peace prevails,
Winter's pulse in soft, sweet trails.

Warmth of hearth, the joy we share,
Moments filled with tender care.
Laughter dances, spirits rise,
In winter's arms, love never dies.

The moon hangs heavy in the night,
Casting dreams in silvery light.
With each breath, we celebrate,
Winter's charm, oh so great.

A Haven in the Cold Embrace

In the stillness, warmth unfolds,
A haven where the heart upholds.
Snowy banks and a bright blue sky,
Together we laugh, together we sigh.

Radiant lights on rooftops gleam,
Woven together, a shared dream.
Fireside tales and whispered lore,
Magic lingers, opening doors.

Chasing shadows, we find delight,
Playing games till the fall of night.
Joy in moments, free as the snow,
In love's sweet embrace, we're free to flow.

The cold may wrap its arms so tight,
But within, there shines a light.
A haven built on love and trust,
In this winter wonder, we must.

Still Waters Beneath Ice

Beneath the ice, the waters gleam,
A world of wonder, like a dream.
Whispers of nature softly call,
In the stillness, we have it all.

Footsteps crunch on a frozen lake,
Reflections shimmer, spirits awake.
A tranquil beauty, calm and bright,
In crisp air, we find delight.

The sun descends with golden rays,
Painting skies in soft arrays.
Gathered warmth, we come alive,
In this serene space, we thrive.

Moments cherished, hearts aligned,
In the still waters, peace we find.
Celebrate the chill, embrace the fun,
In winter's arms, we become one.

Serenity in a Frozen Landscape

Snowflakes dance in playful glee,
Blankets of white embrace the trees.
Laughter fills the frosty air,
Joy and warmth are everywhere.

Candles glow with soft, warm light,
Stars above, a stunning sight.
Carols sung with hearts so bright,
A festive cheer, pure delight.

Children's voices rise in cheer,
As winter's magic draws us near.
Glistening paths of silver grace,
In this sweet and tranquil place.

In harmony, we gather round,
Happiness in every sound.
Unified in pure embrace,
Serenity takes its place.

The Stillness of White

The world is wrapped in soft, white sheets,
Whispers of joy in the snowy streets.
Softly falling, flakes descend,
A wintry tale that will not end.

Children bundled, play and laugh,
Creating memories, their true craft.
Snowmen rise with hats and cheer,
Each gentle voice, a melody dear.

Lights adorn each window sill,
Magic dances, and hearts are still.
The beauty of this festive scene,
A day of peace, calm and serene.

In every heart, warmth does glow,
As the chilly breezes blow.
Here we gather, love unfolds,
In this wonderland of gold.

Frosted Dreams and Gentle Hues

Frosted dreams in shades so bright,
Whispers under the moonlight.
The world aglow with festive cheer,
In every smile, joy appears.

Gentle hues of blue and gold,
The magic of winter, a tale retold.
Laughter echoes through the night,
Hearts are full, spirits take flight.

Candles flicker, warmth surrounds,
A gathering of love abounds.
Songs of joy fill the air,
Every moment, joy to share.

In frosted dreams, we find our way,
Through the night, into the day.
Together here, we find our peace,
In friendship's glow, our joys increase.

Tranquil Blankets of Silence

Tranquil blankets of silence laid,
Underneath the stars, dreams are weighed.
In the hush, a promise thrives,
Where the spirit of joy arrives.

Icicles twinkle like gems so rare,
Nature's canvas, beyond compare.
Every heartbeat, a song refined,
In the stillness, all aligned.

Families gather, laughter rings,
The warmth of love, the joy it brings.
Through the crispness of frosty air,
A celebration beyond compare.

With hearts entwined, we share this night,
In the soft glow of candlelight.
As winter wraps us in its grace,
In every smile, a warm embrace.

Solace under the Snowy Cover

Snowflakes dance upon the breeze,
Blanketing the earth with ease.
Children laugh, their spirits high,
Beneath the pale and frosty sky.

Warm fires flicker, stories shared,
In this season, all are paired.
Mugs of cocoa, laughter bright,
Love and joy fill the night.

Footprints trace the silent ground,
In each heart, sweet peace is found.
Winter's chill, a cozy friend,
In this moment, time won't end.

Frosted Reflections of Still Moments

Mirrors of ice, a glittering sheen,
Nature's canvas, pure and serene.
Footsteps crunch on paths of white,
Whispers echo, soft delight.

Glistening trees in crystal attire,
Sparkling dreams, we dare to aspire.
Winter's breath, a gentle sigh,
Painting visions, sweet and spry.

Candles aglow in the twilight hour,
Ember's warmth, a cherished power.
Gathered close, our hearts align,
In frosted moments, we feel divine.

A Realm of Winter's Quiet Glow

A hush blankets the tranquil land,
As snowflakes twirl, a soft command.
Stars peek through the velvet night,
Casting spells of purest light.

Glowing fires break the chill,
Inviting peace, a tranquil thrill.
Carols float on frosty air,
Joyful hearts, beyond compare.

In this realm of tranquil dreams,
Everything sparkles, or so it seems.
Holding close what matters most,
In winter's magic, we all boast.

The Silent Symphony of Crystal Flakes

Crystal flakes, a symphony vast,
Whispers of winter, shadows cast.
Each flake echoes a soft refrain,
In this season, joy we gain.

Ornaments twinkle on pine trees,
Breezes carry sweet memories.
Gifts exchanged with smiles so wide,
In this warmth, our hearts abide.

With every flake, a story told,
In silent moments, love unfolds.
Gathered around, our voices sing,
In winter's charm, our spirits take wing.

Echoes of Silence on Frosted Ground

A sparkle glints beneath the trees,
Soft whispers ride on the winter breeze.
Footprints weave through drifts of white,
In this stillness, pure delight.

Laughter breaks the quiet night,
As stars above shine oh so bright.
Fires crackle, warm and near,
In this season, joy is here.

The chill wraps 'round like a friendly hug,
As we gather close, a warm tug.
Hearts beat in a rhythmic sound,
In the echoes on the frosted ground.

Shadows of Peace Beneath the Moon

The moonlight bathes the earth in glow,
Casting shadows, soft and slow.
Whispers float on the night air,
In this moment, free from care.

Candles flicker, dance and sway,
Guiding spirits on their way.
Lulled by calm, we gently sway,
In the peace that night conveys.

Harmonies of laughter sing,
To the joy that winter brings.
Underneath this silver dome,
In the shadows, we find home.

The Gentle Mantle of Winter's Care

A blanket white covers the land,
Soft and gentle, nature's hand.
Every flake, a work of art,
A brush of love, to warm the heart.

Families gather, warmth abounds,
With stories shared, in joyful sounds.
Cocoa steams, and spirits rise,
Embracing warmth beneath the skies.

With laughter bright, and cheer awake,
We cherish every memory we make.
Wrapped in love, no burdens bear,
In the gentle mantle of winter's care.

Dreaming in a Frost-kissed Reality

In dreams of snowflakes, I do soar,
To lands where winter opens doors.
With every flurry, whispers call,
In frost-kissed realms, I stand tall.

Glistening paths lead me to roam,
In this wonderland, I feel at home.
The night is alive with crystal light,
In the beauty of a wintry night.

Each breath forms clouds in the chill,
As I dance, my heart is still.
In slumber's grace, I know it's true,
In this reality, I find my cue.

Chasing Shadows in the Winter Light

In the glow of the sun, shadows dance,
Children laughing, lost in a trance.
Snowflakes swirl like twinkling stars,
Joyful moments, no need for scars.

Colorful lights twinkle on trees,
Warming hearts with the winter breeze.
Cookies baking, the smell so sweet,
Gather around, let love repeat.

Sleds racing down the hills with cheer,
Voices echo, spreading good cheer.
Every face aglow with delight,
Chasing shadows in the winter light.

The Embrace of White Wonder

Blankets of snow cover the town,
A magical hush, a soft white gown.
Laughter spills from every home,
In this wonderland, we freely roam.

Candles flicker in windows bright,
Each flicker shares a spark of light.
Families gather, tales unfold,
Woven together, memories gold.

Snowmen rise with hats and scarves,
Joyful creations, love's warm harves.
The world aglow, a charming sight,
In the embrace of white wonder, pure delight.

Solitary Footprints in a Flurry

Footprints trail where few have walked,
In shimmering snow, secrets unlocked.
Every step whispers a new tale,
As winter winds begin to wail.

The air is crisp with a festive flair,
Nature's canvas, painted with care.
Each track leads to moments divine,
In solitude's dance, we brightly shine.

Frosty branches against the blue,
A world renewed, refreshed and true.
In the quiet, spirits lift and soar,
Solitary footprints, yet we're never poor.

The Breath of Frost-kissed Air

Whispers of winter, the air feels bright,
Every breath carries joy and delight.
The world breathes softly, a lullaby,
As snowflakes spiral down from the sky.

Huddled close, we share warm tea,
In laughter's embrace, we feel so free.
Voices sing through the brisk night air,
Creating bonds that we all can share.

Firelight dances, shadows play,
In the warmth of love, we choose to stay.
With every inhale, we find our way,
In the breath of frost-kissed air, we sway.

Frosted Dreams in Silent Night

In the glow of twinkling lights,
Joy dances in the air,
Children's laughter echoes bright,
As winter dreams beyond compare.

Snowflakes swirl like whispered songs,
Covering the world so white,
In this moment, nothing's wrong,
Frosted dreams in silent night.

Warmth of cocoa, mugs in hand,
Stories shared by crackling fire,
In this cozy, winter land,
Hearts are lifted, spirits higher.

As the stars begin to twinkle,
And the moon glows soft and bright,
We'll embrace the magic's sprinkle,
In frosted dreams of silent night.

Embracing the Chill of Solace

The air is crisp, the world aglow,
Footprints dance on frosted ground,
Winter whispers, soft and slow,
In every flake, pure joy is found.

Bundled tight in scarves of hue,
We venture forth, hearts open wide,
With every breath, a chill so true,
In nature's solace, we abide.

Sledding down the hills of white,
Laughter ringing, pure delight,
Underneath the pale moon's light,
Embracing winter's sweet insight.

Shimmering trees, a sight divine,
With ornaments from seasons past,
Together, we will intertwine,
In this chill, our memories cast.

Winter's Gentle Heartbeat

The world adorned in icy lace,
Crickets hush and silence sings,
Nature pauses, slow embrace,
In this wonder, joy it brings.

Gentle flakes like feathers fall,
Whispers soft as velvet night,
Winter's heartbeat, calm and small,
Wrapping all in pure delight.

Woodsmoke curling, fires aglow,
Stories shared, the warmth we feel,
In winter's arms, love's gentle flow,
Life's simple joys, the heart's ideal.

As the year begins to fade,
Embers glow in darkest hour,
In this stillness, dreams are made,
Winter's gentle, soothing power.

The Stillness of a Snow-Laden Sky

Beneath a sky of muted gray,
Snowflakes waltz in soft descent,
A gentle hush, the world at play,
In winter's glow, our hearts are lent.

Branches heavy, dressed in white,
Whispers soft, a tranquil sigh,
In the stillness, pure delight,
Underneath this snow-laden sky.

Candles flicker, casting cheer,
Homes are filled with warmth and love,
As winter wraps us, drawing near,
In every heart, a song above.

This festive mood, a time to share,
Traditions kept, as memories fly,
In joyful times, we find our pair,
Lost in wonder beneath the sky.

Shimmering Peace Beneath the Stars

Twinkling lights adorn the sky,
Joyful laughter, spirits fly.
Hearts aglow, we gather near,
Warming wishes, spreading cheer.

Candles flicker, soft and bright,
As we dance through the night.
Stories shared, love's embrace,
In this sacred, festive space.

Chorus of voices, sweet and clear,
Ringing softly in our ear.
Hope and peace, our wishes blend,
In this moment, hearts transcend.

With every star, our dreams ignite,
Underneath this wondrous light.
Together, we craft a tale,
Of joy and love, we shall not fail.

The Hushed Glow of January

A quiet hush, the world in white,
January's glow, pure delight.
Snowflakes dancing, softly spin,
Nature's canvas, fresh begin.

Cozy fires, the warmth of home,
In the cold, we safely roam.
Kindred souls gather tight,
In this season, hearts feel light.

With every sip of cocoa sweet,
Joyful memories we repeat.
As the evenings gently fade,
In our hearts, a serenade.

January sings a tender song,
In its charm, we all belong.
Beneath the glow, we share a dream,
Life's a tapestry, a shimmering theme.

A Retreat into Frosted Stillness

Whispers soft, the world at bay,
Frosted branches, white and gray.
In the stillness, time stands still,
Nature's breath, a tranquil thrill.

Blankets warm, a cherished view,
Each moment shared, pure and true.
Winter's hush, a gentle spell,
Invites our hearts to share and dwell.

Outside, the world wears a crown,
Of silvery dreams, a soft gown.
In this retreat, we intertwine,
With peace that sparkles, truly divine.

Hear the silence, joys unfold,
In this moment, we behold.
Frosted stillness, so sublime,
In every heartbeat, love's sweet rhyme.

Veils of Silence Among the Drifts

Veils of silence drape the night,
Amidst the drifts, a soft white light.
Snowflakes fall, like whispers shared,
In this stillness, love is bared.

Footsteps echo, soft and low,
In the quiet, joy will grow.
Gathered close, we warm our hearts,
In this moment, life imparts.

With each laughter, spirits soar,
Amidst the drifts, we seek for more.
Open arms, a welcome here,
In unity, we cast out fear.

Veils of silence, stars align,
We find our peace, a love divine.
Underneath this night so bright,
We share our dreams, hearts take flight.

A Mosaic of Crystalized Calm

In the stillness, snowflakes dance,
Each a gem, caught in a glance.
Laughter echoes through the trees,
As joy whispers in the breeze.

Colors twinkle, lights aglow,
A tapestry of joy to show.
Families gather, hearts so bright,
Wrapped in warmth, a pure delight.

Heartfelt stories shared at night,
Under stars, a wondrous sight.
With every cheer, a bond we weave,
In this moment, we believe.

As the world is dressed in white,
We find peace in this soft light.
A mosaic of love and cheer,
In crystal calm, all hold dear.

Threads of Peace in Chilled Air

Beneath the blanket of the night,
The moon glows with a gentle light.
Frosted whispers gently call,
A chorus sweet, embracing all.

Children play with glowing eyes,
Throwing laughter to the skies.
Each moment wrapped like a gift,
In this season, hearts can lift.

Crisp air dances, breath so clear,
Overviewing joys that draw us near.
Hand in hand, we find our way,
Through this magic of the day.

Through every thread of peace we share,
We find solace in the air.
United under stars so bright,
In our hearts, a warm light.

The Embrace of Frost and Quiet

Evening falls, a soft embrace,
Frosted dreams, a tranquil space.
Whispers carry on the breeze,
Nature sleeping, hearts at ease.

Glowing fires, crackling cheer,
In the quiet, love is near.
Glistening branches shimmer bright,
Capturing magic of the night.

Harmony in every breath,
Celebrating life and death.
In the stillness, joy takes wing,
As we gather, sweet songs to sing.

In the embrace of frost, we find,
A kinship strong, a heart aligned.
Together through the winter's chill,
We forge memories, time stands still.

Starlit Moments in the Winter's Keep

Under starlit skies we roam,
In this season, we find home.
Snowflakes twirl in dazzling flight,
Creating magic, pure delight.

Candles flicker, shadows play,
Leading hearts along the way.
Stories shared around the fire,
Igniting dreams and sweet desire.

In the winter's cozy hold,
Friendship's warmth, a treasure gold.
With every laugh and each embrace,
We find pure joy in every space.

Moments cherished, hearts entwined,
Together, every joy combined.
In our laughter, love runs deep,
In starlit moments, memories keep.

Muffled Footsteps of Serenity

The snowflakes dance, a gentle swirl,
In winter's breath, the soft winds unfurl.
Beneath the sky, stars twinkle bright,
Muffled footsteps lead into the night.

Joyful laughter echoes all around,
As hearts align with the magic found.
With warm embraces and cheer so pure,
The spirit of peace we all ensure.

Candles flicker with a golden glow,
As dreams ignite in the falling snow.
Together we gather, side by side,
In this serene moment, hearts open wide.

With every laugh and whispered cheer,
We hold the warmth of love so near.
In every heart, a glowing ember,
Muffled footsteps, a joy to remember.

Glimmers of Light Through Shimmering Ice

Beneath a cloak of winter's sheen,
Glimmers of light emerge, serene.
The world transformed by frosty breath,
Ice crystals dance, enchanting, blessed.

Each branch adorned with glittering lace,
Nature's beauty, an endless embrace.
Reflecting warmth in the coldest night,
A radiant glow, a hopeful light.

Children's laughter fills the air,
As joy ignites, without a care.
They chase the sparkles, innocent plays,
In this festive realm, where magic stays.

As we share stories, laughter flows,
Under the moonlight, love brightly glows.
In the heart of winter's dreamlike skies,
We find our bliss, with glimmering eyes.

Silent Elegance Amongst the Pines

Amongst the pines, a tranquil grace,
Silent elegance in this sacred space.
Whispers of snow weave through the trees,
In harmony, carried by the breeze.

A blanket of white cloaks the ground,
A serene path where peace is found.
The world pauses for a gentle sigh,
Under the branches, we wander by.

Candles aglow in the evening's hush,
Invite us softly to gather and trust.
With hearts afire in the calm of night,
We share our hopes with the fading light.

In each moment, a soft embrace,
A gathering spot, a cherished place.
Amongst the pines, we feel the call,
Silent elegance, a gift to us all.

Frosted Reflections in the Quiet Night

The night descends with a peaceful hush,
Frosted reflections in the moonlit rush.
Gentle whispers glide on the breeze,
As time stands still, our hearts find ease.

Stars shimmer bright in the velvet sky,
A tapestry woven, where dreams can fly.
In every breath, the magic we share,
With hopes and wishes hanging in the air.

As laughter rings through the crisp night air,
We weave our tales, a bond laid bare.
Within this solace, we find delight,
Frosted reflections, a festive sight.

With every twinkling light we see,
A reminder of love's sweet decree.
In the quiet night, our spirits soar,
Frosted reflections, forevermore.

When Time Falls Silent

In the glow of twinkling lights,
Laughter echoes through the air,
Moments cherished, hearts take flight,
A festive spirit everywhere.

Candles flicker, shadows dance,
Gathered close, we share a toast,
Joyous hearts in sweet romance,
Together here, we love the most.

Snowflakes drift like whispers soft,
As winter tales begin to weave,
In this magic, we lift off,
With dreams we dare to believe.

When time falls silent, smiles proclaim,
The joy of seasons, bright and wide,
In this moment, we find our flame,
Together here, with hearts as guide.

A Symphony of Ice and Silence

Glittering snow, a wondrous sight,
Crystalline dreams on frosty ground,
Nature dons her veil of white,
In silence, magic can be found.

Echoes of laughter fill the night,
Around the fire, warm and bright,
Stories shared, a sweet delight,
As stars above begin to light.

A symphony plays, hush and sweet,
As ice and snow in chorus blend,
We dance to rhythms soft and neat,
In every heart, the joy we send.

With each embrace and fleeting glance,
We weave together warmth and cheer,
In winter's wondrous, frosty dance,
A celebration, crystal clear.

Beneath the Quiet Veil

Underneath the quiet veil,
Snowflakes whisper, secrets told,
A world adorned in frosty pale,
In the stillness, we behold.

Gathered friends, a circle bright,
In the warmth of love we dwell,
Through the magic of the night,
Casting dreams beneath the spell.

Each joyful cheer, a shooting star,
Lighting paths with hearts aglow,
Beneath the moon, we wander far,
In this embrace, we let love grow.

A festive spirit fills the air,
With every laugh and smile we share,
In this moment, free from care,
Together found, a bond so rare.

Tranquil Moments in a White Landscape

In the hush of winter's breath,
Peaceful echoes fill the space,
Moments linger, sweet as death,
In this white, embracing place.

Children's laughter, crisp and bright,
As snowflakes dance on frozen lakes,
In the glow of festive light,
Joyous hearts, the world awakes.

Hot cocoa warms our hands so tight,
Fires crackle, stories bloom,
With friends and family, pure delight,
We gather close to chase the gloom.

Tranquil moments shared as one,
In this winter's soft embrace,
As day gives way to setting sun,
We find our joy in every trace.

Lullaby Beneath the Frost

In the hush of night, stars gleam bright,
Snowflakes dance, a soft delight.
Whispers of joy fill the frozen air,
Children's laughter, everywhere.

Moonlight spills like silver dreams,
Fires crackle, warming themes.
Together we sing in the gentle glow,
Wrapped in warmth from head to toe.

Pine trees swayed with twinkling lights,
Each breath taken, with pure delight.
Ode to the season, so sweet and clear,
We celebrate this time of year.

Sleigh bells ring, a merry sound,
In this magic, love is found.
Under blankets, snug and tight,
Beneath the frost, all is bright.

A Crystal Veil of Solitude

In a world so still, beneath the sky,
Snowflakes descend, a quiet sigh.
Wrapped in crystal, the earth sleeps,
As secrets hold what winter keeps.

Morning light brings a jeweled glow,
Each leaf adorned in glistening snow.
Footprints left in patterns neat,
Breathe the freshness, feel the beat.

Solitude dances between the trees,
A tranquil moment in the freeze.
With every sparkle, memories rise,
Under a cloak of muted ties.

Sipping cocoa by the fire's light,
The world outside, pure and white.
In this stillness, hearts can roam,
In a crystal veil, we find our home.

Echoes of a Snowy Silence

Beneath the falling, silken white,
The world pauses, lost in light.
Voices hushed, a tranquil tone,
In snowy silence, we find our own.

Branches bow with the weight of snow,
Nature's stillness, a soft glow.
Each flake a story, whispered low,
In this quiet, emotions flow.

Gentle breezes weave through the trees,
A melody carried on winter's freeze.
Underneath the sky so grand,
We gather close, hand in hand.

Stars awaken, twinkling bright,
Sharing secrets of the night.
In snowy silence, dreams take flight,
Creating joy till morning light.

The Tranquil Shroud

A tranquil shroud of white descends,
Cocooning earth, as winter bends.
Time stands still, the world aglow,
In this beauty, let spirits flow.

Whispers of peace in the air we share,
Every breath taken, without a care.
Sleds and laughter from hilltops high,
In pure delight, we touch the sky.

Candlelight flickers against the dark,
Warm embraces, a loving spark.
Gathered close, with stories old,
In this season, dreams unfold.

Snowflakes flutter, a gentle kiss,
Promising moments of eternal bliss.
With joy, we welcome winter's song,
In harmony, we all belong.

Frosted Memories of Solace

In chilly air, we gather round,
With laughter bright, our joys abound.
The frost dances on each merry face,
In this warm hearted, shared embrace.

Windows gleam with twinkling light,
As stories weave through snowy night.
We sip hot cocoa, watching flurries fall,
Our frost-kissed memories forever call.

With every smile, our spirits soar,
Celebrating love, who could ask for more?
The festive cheer, it fills the space,
Forever etched in this special place.

A toast to warmth, to friendships true,
In this frosted moment, I find you.
Our hearts unite, a glowing art,
In tranquil peace, we never part.

Whispers of Nature's Rest

Amidst the woods where silence sings,
Nature slumbers, wrapped in wings.
A festive hush covers the land,
In snowflakes' dance, life makes its stand.

The brook whispers tales of the past,
Each crystal flake, a wonder cast.
Underneath the starry dome,
The frosty air feels much like home.

With every step, the crunching sound,
Echoes softly, joy unbound.
Nature's lullaby calls us near,
In the cool embrace, we cast out fear.

In whispered breaths, the world slows down,
Among the trees, we softly crown.
With spirits high, and hearts so blessed,
We relish in nature's gentle rest.

Candles Flickering Against the Chill

Candles flicker, casting glow,
Against the chill, a warmth we know.
Their gentle light, like stars above,
Illuminates the paths of love.

Gathered close, we share our dreams,
In laughter's song, our spirit beams.
The air is rich with scents divine,
As festive joy in hearts entwine.

Each flame a promise, bright and true,
In this cozy warmth, we find the new.
The cold outside, it can't compare,
To the joy found in this care.

So here we stand, in flickering light,
Embracing love, wrapping it tight.
In every laugh, in every thrill,
Our hearts unite, despite the chill.

Lullabies Wrapped in White

Snow blankets softly, a gentle quilt,
In this winter wonderland we've built.
With wonders wrapped in silver hue,
Each flake a gift, both fresh and new.

Lullabies drift on the whispering breeze,
As time stands still among the trees.
Carols float from hearts so light,
In this magical, wintry night.

With every twinkle, joy appears,
In merry whispers, we conquer fears.
Nature sings as the moon does rise,
Wrapped in white, beneath starlit skies.

We dance through dreams, our spirits soar,
In festive joy, forevermore.
With lullabies echoing through the night,
Wrapped in warmth, our futures bright.

A Haven Wrapped in White

Snowflakes dance in candlelight,
Joyful laughter fills the night.
Families gather, hearts align,
Wrapped in warmth, the stars will shine.

Candles glow on windowsills,
Chasing away the midnight chills.
With each hug, a story shared,
In this haven, love declared.

Outside, the world is dressed in white,
Inside, our spirits soar in flight.
Hot cocoa swirls in every cup,
Embracing the warmth that lifts us up.

In this moment, time stands still,
Winter's magic, a gentle thrill.
A haven found, where dreams ignite,
Together we shine, forever bright.

Crystal Slumbers Beneath the Sage

Underneath the silver sky,
Crystals glimmer, softly nigh.
Whispers fill the frosty air,
Nature sleeping, dreams laid bare.

Moonlight graces the sage's arms,
Luring us with its quiet charms.
Wrapped in blankets of frosty white,
We find warmth in winter's night.

Each twig sparkles, dreams take flight,
The hush of stillness, pure delight.
Gentle shadows, softly swayed,
In this garden, peace is laid.

Bringing forth a tranquil spell,
Tales of winter, hearts compel.
Together, we rest, side by side,
In crystal slumbers, where hope abides.

Peaceful Blankets of Serenity

Softly wrapped in layers tight,
Peace descends with gentle might.
Snowflakes fall, a tender kiss,
Blanketing the world in bliss.

Moonbeams bathe the silent earth,
Welcoming a time of mirth.
With each breath, the stillness grows,
In peaceful blanket, warmth bestows.

Children play, their laughter sweet,
Building dreams with dancing feet.
Moments cherished, hearts unite,
Under stars that twinkle bright.

Fires crackle, stories flow,
In this haven, love will grow.
Serenity wraps us in its fold,
As winter's wonders, we behold.

Echoes of Calm in Winter's Grasp

In winter's grasp, the world feels pure,
Echoes of calm, a soothing cure.
Whispers float on frosty air,
Filling hearts with joy and care.

Shimmering lights adorn the trees,
Carried softly on the breeze.
Gathered close, lamplight gleams,
Warming souls and kindling dreams.

Quiet moments, we hold dear,
A season rich with love and cheer.
Through swirling snow, we dance and play,
In winter's calm, we find our way.

With every heartbeat, peace cascades,
Among the glimmers, the silence wades.
Echoes linger, spirits rise,
Beneath the vast and starry skies.

Quietude Among the Icebound Trees

Whispers of joy in the frosty air,
Crystal branches glistening everywhere.
Laughter echoes, pure and clear,
Hearts are warm, despite the chill here.

Snowflakes dance, a gentle ballet,
Children play in the bright array.
Each breath a cloud, a moment to seize,
Wrapped in magic among the trees.

Fires crackle with stories to share,
Hot cocoa warms the hands in the square.
Faces aglow in the twinkling light,
A festive embrace in the still of night.

Nature's beauty unfolds in white,
A canvas sparkling, pure delight.
Together we gather, our spirits free,
In the quietude, we find harmony.

Harmony in a World of White

Songs of joy drift on the breeze,
Footprints mark paths through the trees.
Frosted breath mingles with laughter,
In this winter, dreams come after.

Candles flicker, casting a glow,
In the twilight, warmth begins to flow.
Friends and family close, no divide,
Together we stand, with hearts open wide.

Snow blankets all in a peaceful grace,
A shimmering veil on each familiar place.
The world is soft, serene, and bright,
In harmony, we greet the night.

Under stars that twinkle above,
We gather, laugh, and share our love.
With each moment, joy intertwines,
In a world of white, the spirit shines.

The Light of a Pale Horizon

Morning breaks with whispers of gold,
A canvas vast, a story unfolds.
The pale horizon beckons us near,
In winter's embrace, we shed our fear.

Glowing embers in a morning frost,
A reminder of warmth, never lost.
With every step, we chase the delight,
In the beauty of a crisp, wintry light.

Birds take flight, a jubilant song,
In soaring arcs, they dance along.
The chill in the air sparks hearts anew,
As laughter shared feels fresh as dew.

In nature's gaze, we find our place,
The light of a pale horizon, our grace.
With every moment, together we thrive,
In winter's glow, we come alive.

Winter's Softest Lullaby

Snow blankets the earth, a soft embrace,
Whispers of peace in this tranquil space.
Stars twinkle gently in the dark,
While dreams drift softly, a tender spark.

Frosty windows frame a warm glow,
Inside, laughter dances, fond and low.
Family gathers, hearts intertwined,
In winter's lullaby, sweetly defined.

Outside, the world slows to a pause,
Nature's beauty leads us to applause.
Each flake a note in this silent tune,
Under the watch of the bright crescent moon.

With cocoa to warm and stories to share,
We find ourselves lost in winter's care.
In the softest lullaby, we reside,
With love and joy as our guiding guide.

The Beauty of a Frosty Silence

Snowflakes dance in the shimmering light,
Covering the earth, a blanket so bright.
Whispers of chill in the crisp, clear air,
In this frosty silence, joy is fair.

Laughter erupts in the glistening night,
As friends gather close, hearts feeling light.
Mugs filled with cocoa, warmth in our hands,
Together we cherish these magical lands.

Stars twinkle down in the velvety sky,
A canvas of dreams where our spirits fly.
The beauty of winter, a wondrous sight,
In frosty silence, the world feels just right.

In the Heart of Winter's Calm

Winter's breath rests on the world so still,
A hush envelops the valley and hill.
Firewood crackles, igniting the glow,
In the heart of winter, our spirits flow.

Frost-kissed branches, a delicate art,
Each icy crystal a work from the heart.
Beneath the moon's gaze, silver and bright,
We gather together, a warm, joyful sight.

Softly we sing with voices so clear,
Echoes of laughter are all that we hear.
In cozy corners, with loved ones so dear,
In the heart of winter, we share our cheer.

Flickers of Warmth in a Frozen World

Fireside chats, where stories ignite,
Flickers of warmth in the chill of the night.
The world outside sparkles with frozen glee,
While we stay together, just you and me.

Scarves wrapped tightly, we venture outside,
With twinkling lights in the evening's tide.
Snowmen and snowballs, our laughter takes flight,
In a frozen world, everything feels right.

Candles glow softly, a flickering dance,
Illuminating moments that sparkle and chance.
With every heartbeat, we bask in the glow,
Flickers of warmth as the cool winds blow.

Tranquil Nights Under an Icy Sky

Under an icy sky, stars gleam above,
A tranquil night filled with wonder and love.
The air is crisp, with a whispering peace,
In this winter's hush, all worries cease.

Gentle snowfalls, a quiet embrace,
Softly they land, a delicate trace.
With hearts intertwined, we stroll hand in hand,
Embracing the beauty of this frozen land.

The world around us, a shimmering glow,
In the stillness of night, our spirits grow.
Enchanted by magic, we surrender to dreams,
Tranquil nights woven with love's gentle seams.

Harvesting Peace in the Chill

In fields of gold where sunbeams play,
We gather joy, our hearts at bay.
The autumn air, so crisp and bright,
Brings hopes anew in morning light.

Children laugh, their voices cheer,
As harvest moons draw ever near.
We dance beneath the starlit skies,
With hearts aglow, our spirits rise.

The basket's full, the bounty shared,
In every hug, in how we cared.
A feast of friendship, love, and grace,
In this bright chill, we find our place.

So raise a glass, let joy ignite,
To peace it brings, this festive night.
We harvest dreams, we sow delight,
In laughter's song, our hearts take flight.

A Tapestry of Rest in the Snow

Blankets white, the world at rest,
Nature sighs, it feels its best.
Under stars that softly gleam,
We gather round, a cozy dream.

With stories shared and fires aglow,
The warmth of hearts begins to flow.
In gentle whispers, we find our way,
Embracing peace on winter's day.

Flakes of white, like lace they fall,
A quiet hush, we hear the call.
Together in this tranquil space,
We weave our hopes, a warm embrace.

So let the cold wind softly blow,
We're wrapped in love, no room for woe.
In this sweet pause, our souls unite,
A tapestry of joy, pure delight.

The Gentle Caress of Winter's Hand

The sky adorned with snowy lace,
A quiet world, a perfect place.
With every breath, the peace flows wide,
Winter's hand, our hearts abide.

Frozen streams that sparkle bright,
Reflect the stars in silent night.
We wander paths where dreams take flight,
In soft embrace of purest white.

All is calm, the world anew,
With every flake, the joy we brew.
Together we savor this time of cheer,
As winter whispers, "Love is near."

So hold your loved ones, near and dear,
In gentle caress, we shed our fear.
Let laughter echo through the land,
In harmony, together we stand.

Dreams Cascading in Crystal Light

Like prisms break, the dawn awakes,
In every heart, a joy that shakes.
Dreams cascade from heights above,
In crystal light, we feel the love.

With bells and songs that fill the air,
We cast aside our every care.
So every smile, like stars ignite,
In vibrant hues, our spirits bright.

Along the lanes where laughter calls,
Through whispered winds, the magic falls.
A symphony of hope and cheer,
In every heart, the world draws near.

Together we'll dance through frosty glow,
Embracing warmth in winter's show.
In dreams that glimmer, shining bright,
We'll find our peace in crystal light.

Whispers of Winter's Embrace

In the stillness, laughter rings,
As icicles shimmer, the cold joy sings.
Warm mittens hug hands, hearts set aglow,
Festive gatherings beneath falling snow.

Twinkling lights adorning each street,
Children's delight, with every soft beat.
Fires flicker, hot cocoa in hand,
Together we bask, as snowflakes do land.

Joyful reunions fill the warm night,
Each whispered secret a flickering light.
The world wrapped in silver, a marvelous sight,
In winter's embrace, the heart feels so right.

With every snowflake, a wish takes flight,
Hope dances softly, pure and so bright.
Together we'll cherish this magical time,
In winter's embrace, our spirits do climb.

A Canvas of Frosted Silence

A glimmering mantle covers the ground,
In silence, the beauty of winter is found.
Footsteps are muffled, the world holds its breath,
Each flake a story, a whisper of depth.

Painted in white, the trees stand so tall,
While shadows of laughter echo through all.
Crisp air is laced with the scent of pine,
In this frost-kissed wonder, joy is divine.

As families gather, warm fires ignite,
The glow of traditions, a heartwarming sight.
With cocoa in hand, we cherish the glow,
In this canvas of silence, our love starts to grow.

Under the moonlight, the stars seem to sway,
Through windows aglow, we watch and we'll play.
With each merry moment, we savor the chill,
Crafting our memories, time stands so still.

Serenity in White Stillness

Snow gently blankets the earth like a dream,
In peaceful repose, all is serene.
Whispers of magic float through the air,
In this winter wonder, we lay our cares bare.

Frost on the window, a delicate art,
Carving the shapes of the joys in our heart.
The night sky adorned in a celestial glow,
Wrapped in the warmth of a crackling fire's flow.

Festivities flourish, as family draws near,
Stories we share, laughter and cheer.
Outside the hush, a world softly glows,
Inside our hearts, a bright love still grows.

With every skater, each child's voice so clear,
In winter's embrace, we gather near.
Serenity dances, adorned with delight,
In the stillness of white, all feels so right.

The Quietude of Blanket Snow

Beneath the stars, the silence is deep,
A blanket of snow, the world watches sleep.
Softly it falls, a gentle white shroud,
In this quietude, we gather proud.

Laughter erupts, as snowballs take flight,
Frosted adventures fill long winter nights.
Mittens and scarves, wrapped snug and tight,
In the magic of winter, our spirits are light.

Glistening rooftops, as bright as the day,
Each home a haven, where children can play.
Echoing joy as the fireplace glows,
Through warmth and togetherness, love surely flows.

As twilight beckons, we gather and sing,
In this tranquil moment, our hearts take wing.
The quietude whispers, our spirits entwine,
In the beauty of snow, all is divine.

The Soft Dance of Falling Feathers

As soft as whispers in the night,
The feathers twirl, pure and bright.
They flutter down like dreams to share,
A festive dance fills the air.

Each one a wish, a joyful treat,
A celebration, light and sweet.
With laughter caught in each descent,
The world is wrapped in joy unspent.

Amidst the glow of lantern light,
We gather close, hearts warm, and bright.
The gentle grace of nature's fling,
A song of peace that makes us sing.

So let us dance, our spirits free,
Inspired by love, in harmony.
With feathers falling all around,
In their embrace, true joy is found.

Beneath the Silver Veil

Beneath the silver veil we play,
In gleaming light, the stars' ballet.
The night is young, and we embrace,
Each twinkle puts a smile on our face.

The moon hangs low, a radiant guide,
With open hearts, we laugh and glide.
The air is sweet with midnight's breeze,
In this calm, we find our ease.

Fireflies dance in joyful arcs,
Igniting dreams like fleeting sparks.
The silver veil, a blanket bright,
Wraps us in warmth, a pure delight.

So let the night be filled with cheer,
As we hold close all we hold dear.
Together, wrapped in dreams we weave;
Beneath this silver veil, we believe.

Frozen Time in Gentle Harmony

In the hush of winter's light,
Frozen time feels soft and bright.
Each flake that falls, a tale to spin,
In gentle harmony, we begin.

The world adorned in white so pure,
A canvas wide, a winter lure.
In laughter shared, the warmth ignites,
As magic weaves through starry nights.

With hearts aglow, we gather 'round,
In every joy, a love profound.
The chill may bite, but spirits soar,
In frozen time, we long for more.

So raise a glass to moments dear,
To frozen time and festive cheer.
Together, let our spirits shine,
In gentle harmony, we're divine.

Nurtured by the Chill

Nurtured by the chill we find,
The magic of a joyful mind.
With every breath, the crisp air sings,
A festive heart, this season brings.

The frosty trees in sparkling glow,
Invite us in to laugh and throw.
In gentle whispers, secrets shared,
A bond of warmth, forever bared.

As we embrace this winter's song,
United, we feel we belong.
Nurtured by the chill's sweet grace,
In this moment, time finds its place.

So gather all, let spirits soar,
For in this chill, we crave much more.
With hearts aglow in Yuletide thrill,
We find our joy, nurtured by the chill.

Serenity in Frozen Breath

Whispers of winter, soft and bright,
Draped in white, a wondrous sight.
Candles flicker, glowing on,
In the chill, the night has drawn.

Laughter dances on the breeze,
Snowflakes twirl from frosty trees.
Joy is shared in every cheer,
Warmth ignites the frosty sphere.

Family gathers, hearts entwine,
As hands embrace with warmth divine.
Every smile, a twinkling star,
In the stillness, we've come far.

Serenity found within the cold,
Memories cherished, stories told.
In frozen breath, our spirits soar,
Festivity thrives forevermore.

A Stillness Renewed by Light

Morning glows on snowy peaks,
Softly whispers, nature speaks.
Glistening crystals, pure and bright,
Awake the world, a fresh delight.

Sparks of joy from every glance,
Each heart rejoices, a merry dance.
Together we share laughter's sound,
In this bliss, our love is found.

Festive feelings, bright and clear,
Embrace the magic of this year.
Hope ignites like warmest fire,
Filling souls with deep desire.

A tapestry woven, golden rays,
In stillness renewed, our spirits play.
The beauty of this endless light,
Ever shines through day and night.

Reflections on a Frigid Canvas

A canvas white, untouched, serene,
Each flake a story, soft and keen.
In silence deep, we find our place,
Reflections dance, a gentle grace.

Moments pause in the frosty air,
Kindred spirits, without a care.
Echoes sweet of laughter's song,
In this stillness, we belong.

Every twinkle, a memory bright,
Frigid canvas filled with light.
Nature's art, a wondrous sight,
Celebrating this winter night.

Together we stroll, hearts in sync,
In sparkling white, we will not blink.
With warmth inside, we lift our voice,
In festive cheer, we all rejoice.

The Dance of Snowflakes in Solitude

Dancing softly, snowflakes fall,
Whirling gently, nature's call.
In the quiet, beauty glows,
As the chilly wind softly blows.

Each flake unique, a pure delight,
Cascading down from heights of white.
We watch in awe, spellbound and still,
As wonder wraps our hearts at will.

In solitude, we find our peace,
A moment captured, fears release.
Together in silence, spirits soar,
As winter's charm opens the door.

Festive spirits rise from below,
In the dance of snowflakes, we flow.
United in joy, we celebrate,
In this stillness, we elevate.